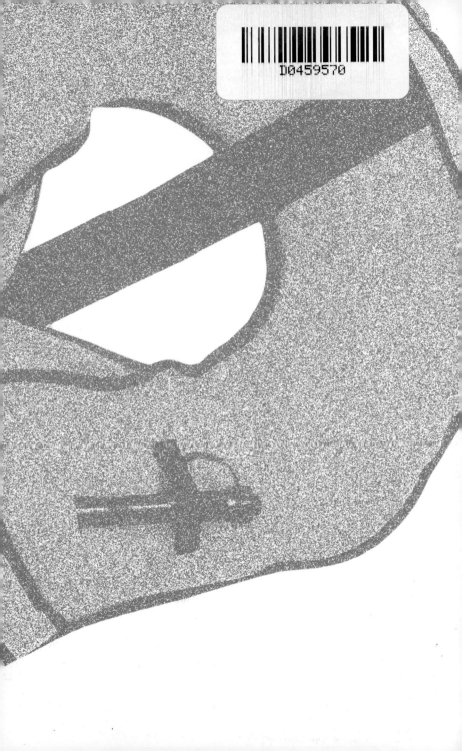

Shipwreck

By Caryn Jenner

Penguin
Random
House

Series Editor Deborah Lock
Project Editor Caryn Jenner
Editor Nandini Gupta
Senior Art Editor Ann Cannings
Art Editor Yamini Panwar
US Senior Editor Shannon Beatty
Producer, Pre-production Francesca Wardell
DTP Designer Anita Yadav, Mohamad Usman
Picture Researcher Deepak Negi
Managing Editor Soma B. Chowdhury
Managing Art Editor Ahlawat Gunjan

Reading Consultant
Linda B. Gambrell, Ph.D.

First American Edition, 2015
Published in the United States by DK Publishing
345 Hudson Street, New York, New York 10014

Copyright © 2015 Dorling Kindersley Limited
A Penguin Random House Company
15 16 17 18 19 10 9 8 7 6 5 4 3 2 1
001—271662—Sept/15

Published in Great Britain by Dorling Kindersley Limited.

A catalog record for this book is available from the Library of Congress.

ISBN: 978-1-4654-3565-1 (Paperback)
ISBN: 978-1-4654-3564-4 (Hardcover)
Printed and bound in China

DK books are available at special discounts when purchased in bulk for sales promotions, premiums, fund-raising,
or educational use. For details, contact: DK Publishing Special Markets, 345 Hudson Street, New York,
New York 10014 or SpecialSales@dk.com.

The publisher would like to thank the following for their kind permission to reproduce their photographs:
(Key: a-above; b-below/bottom; c-center; f-far; l-left; r-right; t-top)
1 Corbis: Konrad Wothe / imageBROKER. **4–5 Dreamstime.com:** Jose Tejo. **4 Dreamstime.com:** Lukasz Frackowiak (bl/used on pg 6bl, 18bl,
20bl, 22bl, 36bl, 38bl, 40bl, 52bl, 54bl, 56bl, 68bl, 70bl, 84bl, 86bl, 88bl, 98bl, 100bl, 112bl, 116bl, 118bl, 120bl, 122bl, 124bl). **5 Dreamstime.
com:** Lukasz Frackowiak (br/used on pg 7br, 19br, 21br, 23br, 37br, 39br, 41br, 53br, 55br, 57br, 69br, 71br, 85br, 87br, 89br, 99br, 101br, 113br,
117br, 119br, 121br, 123br, 125br). **18–19 Dorling Kindersley:** Courtesy of Southern Skirmish Association. **20–21 Punchstock:** Digital
Vision/Tim Hibo. **22–23 Corbis:** Seth Resnick / Science Faction. **24–25 Corbis:** 145 / Images Etc Ltd / Ocean. **26–27 Corbis:** Heritage
Images. **28 Dreamstime.com:** Cory Thoman (tl). **29 Dreamstime.com:** Cory Thoman (tl). **32–33 Dreamstime.com:** Bcbounders. **34–35 Getty
Images:** Monty Rakusen. **36–37 Corbis:** Mitsuaki Iwago / Minden Pictures. **38–39 Dreamstime.com:** Yuliya Belenkova. **38 Dreamstime.com:**
Vasyl Duda (tl). **39 Dreamstime.com:** Algol (t). **40 Dreamstime.com:** Artshock (tl). **44–45 Corbis:** Seth Resnick / Science Faction.
47 Dorling Kindersley: Linda Pitkin. **48–49 Dreamstime.com:** Taiga. **50 Alamy Images:** david gregs (crb). **Getty Images:** King Don (bl).
iStockphoto.com: DanBrandenburg (cl). **51 Dreamstime.com:** Joseph Gough (t). **52–53 Dreamstime.com:** Gentoomultimedia. **54–55
Dorling Kindersley:** Dan Bannister. **56–57 Dreamstime.com:** Vilainecrevette. **60–61 Dreamstime.com:** Molly70photo. **64 Dreamstime.com:**
Les Cunliffe (t, b). **65 Dreamstime.com:** Les Cunliffe (t, c). **66 Dreamstime.com:** Philcold (tl). **68 Corbis.** **70–71 Dreamstime.com:** Joseph
Gough. **72 Corbis:** Sergio Pitamitz / Robert Harding World Imagery (t/window). **73 Corbis:** Sergio Pitamitz / Robert Harding World Imagery
(b/window). Seth Resnick / Science Faction (b). **74–75 Dreamstime.com:** Zacarias Pereira Da Mata. **77 NASA:** MODIS Rapid Response
team (t). **78 Corbis:** Demotix sourced / Demotix (cla); Zahidul Karim Salim / NurPhoto / NurPhoto (crb). **79 Corbis:** Bagus Indahono / epa
(cb); Mike Theiss / Ultimate Chase (tl); STR / Reuters (cra). **80–81 Dreamstime.com:** Rozaliya. **84 Dreamstime.com:** Pavel Losevsky (b).
86–87 Corbis: Jane / fstop. **92 Dreamstime.com:** Luckydoor (cr); Christoph Weihs (tl); Denise Peillon (br). **93 Dreamstime.com:** Per
Björkdahl (cr, bl). **94 Dreamstime.com:** Denis Dubrovin (c). **96 Dreamstime.com:** Georgios Kollidas (tl). **96–97 Dreamstime.com:** Kellydt.
97 Alamy Images: Chris Hellier (cra). **98–99 Alamy Images:** Mike Hill. **102–103 Dreamstime.com:** Brian Grant. **108–109 Corbis:** Stuart
Westmorland Photography / Image Source. **110–111 Corbis:** Radius Images. **120 Dreamstime.com:** Denis Dubrovin (crb); Gloria Rosazza
(tc). **NASA:** Jesse Allen, Earth Observatory (clb). **121 Dreamstime.com:** Cory Thoman (cla); Denis Dubrovin (clb, cb).
Getty Images: Gail Shumway (bl).
Jacket images: Front: Getty Images: artpartner images / The Image Bank. **Back: Corbis:** Mitsuaki Iwago / Minden Pictures.
Spine: Dorling Kindersley: Brice Minnigh / Rough Guides.

All other images © Dorling Kindersley
For further information see: www.dkimages.com

A WORLD OF IDEAS:
SEE ALL THERE IS TO KNOW
www.dk.com

CONTENTS

4 Shipwreck!

6 Parts of a Ship

8 **Chapter 1** Voyages of Doom

30 **Chapter 2** Ships

44 **Chapter 3** Oceans and Seas

68 **Chapter 4** Weather at Sea

82 **Chapter 5** Survival at Sea

98 **Chapter 6** Animal Heroes

112 **Chapter 7** Exploring Shipwrecks

120 Surviving at Sea Game

122 Shipwreck Quiz

124 Glossary

126 Index

127 About the Author and Consultant

Shipwreck!

The remains of this boat lie on the bottom of the Caribbean Sea. How did it sink? When? Who was on board? Did they survive? Some shipwrecks have been thoroughly investigated, but others remain mysteries....

Parts of a Ship

Before you find out more about shipwrecks, it's important to know some basic parts of a ship.

The stern is the rear of the ship.

As you face the bow, the right side of the ship is the starboard side.

As you face the bow, the left side of the ship is the port side.

The bow is the front of the ship.

The hull is the main body of the ship.

Chapter 1

Voyages of Doom

When you board a boat or a ship and sail out into the ocean, you always hope for a smooth voyage with sunny skies and calm seas. You think the worst that might happen is that you might feel a little seasick. You certainly wouldn't expect the voyage to end in shipwreck.

TITANIC

Many people believed that the *Titanic* was unsinkable. Yet just four days into its one and only voyage in 1912, the luxury liner plunged to the ocean floor. The truth is, there is no such thing as an unsinkable ship. Shortly after it was called "unsinkable," the *Titanic* was sailing from Southampton, England, to New York City when it scraped against an iceberg in the north Atlantic Ocean. Water poured in through a series of gashes in the hull. About 1,500 people went down with the ship.

Along with the tragic circumstances, one reason for the public's fascination with the *Titanic* is that we have a lot of information about the ship and some of the survivors have given detailed accounts of their experiences. This makes it easier to picture the details of what happened, and to wonder what if circumstances had been different?

THE SINKING OF THE **TITANIC**

On April 10, 1912, the *Titanic* **set sail on its maiden (first) voyage from Southampton, England, bound for New York City. It was a large, luxurious ship and people said it was "unsinkable." The trip was expected to take one week.**

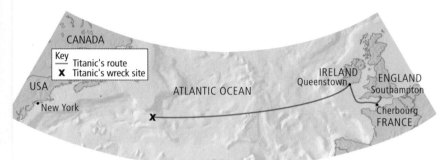

The night of April 14 was clear and cold. The sea was calm. The *Titanic* was sailing at full speed. At about 11:40 pm, lookout Frederick Fleet, who was keeping watch from high up in the crow's nest, spotted an iceberg ahead and rang the warning bell. First Officer William Murdoch was in charge of the ship at the time. He told Quartermaster Robert Hichens to turn the ship's wheel, but the huge liner couldn't avoid the iceberg. The *Titanic* struck the iceberg on the starboard (right) side of the hull.

The collision only caused minor damage to the upper decks, but below the surface of the sea, the iceberg punched a series of gashes and holes along the hull, which started filling up with water. Just after midnight, Captain Edward Smith gave the order to abandon ship.

Within three hours, the *Titanic* sank. Sadly, more than 1,500 people died, due to a lack of safety procedures and a shortage of lifeboats on the "unsinkable" *Titanic*.

VASA

In 1628, Sweden's finest warship, the *Vasa*, was ready for her maiden voyage. However, the *Vasa* had sailed only about 4,500 feet (1,500 m) out of the harbor at the Swedish capital of Stockholm when a sudden gust of wind filled the sails and the ship tipped over onto its side. The gunports had been left open to show off the ship's gleaming new armory, and water gushed in. The *Vasa* flooded and sank in 115 feet (35 m) of water. Only the tops of the masts were left poking above the surface.

The *Vasa* had been poorly designed. It was top-heavy with guns and there was not enough heavy material on the lower decks to keep the ship stable. When the wind blew, the *Vasa* was knocked off balance and over it went.

The restored *Vasa* at the museum in Stockholm

Cannons aiming
out of the
gunports

In 1664, 53 of the
Vasa's 64 cannons were
recovered, but as the masts
rotted and fell into the sea,
the rest of the ship was abandoned.
Then, in 1956, the Swedish government
decided to raise the *Vasa*. In 1961, the
Vasa emerged after 333 years beneath the
sea. About 15,000 objects were also
recovered. These ranged from the huge
sails that were stored in the *Vasa's* sail
locker, to intricately carved wooden
figures and ornaments that were part
of the ship's decoration. There were also

seamen's chests packed with leather boots
and felt hats. Even a tub of butter was
found! The bones of 25 people were also
discovered. The *Vasa* was restored to her
former glory and visitors could finally
see the ship on display at a specially built
museum in Stockholm.

ARCTIC AND VESTA

In 1854, a liner called the *Arctic* was sailing from England to New York when it came across thick fog about 62 miles (100 km) from the American coast. Ignoring the fog, Captain Luce continued to sail full speed ahead. Suddenly, he saw a dark shape heading right toward the *Arctic*.

Through the fog came another ship, the *Vesta*. It was too late for either vessel to change course. The *Vesta* crashed straight into the *Arctic's* side! At first, Captain Luce thought the damage to the *Arctic* was limited and he carried on toward the nearest port, leaving the *Vesta* to its fate.

Damage to the *Vesta* seemed much worse. The ship was quickly taking on water. Captain Duchesne and his crew started throwing cargo overboard to lighten the ship. It worked! The bow lifted far enough out of the water so that the ship could continue.

When the *Vesta* limped into port several days later, the captain and crew discovered that the *Arctic* had never made it back! Three large holes in the *Arctic's* hull had filled up with water. At last, Captain Luce gave the order to abandon ship, but sadly, there weren't enough lifeboats for everyone.

Out of 435 people on board the *Arctic*, only 85 survived. One of the survivors was Captain Luce, who spent two days clinging to wreckage before being rescued. Too late, he realized that if he had stayed to help the *Vesta*, the *Arctic* might have been saved as well.

?

What decision did Captain Luce make that decided the fate of the *Arctic*?

SS REPUBLIC

In 1865, the *SS Republic* steamship was on its way from New York City to New Orleans, Louisiana, when it hit a deadly hurricane off the east coast of the United States! Amazingly, the passengers and crew managed to escape, but the ship's cargo, including valuable silver and gold coins, sank with the *SS Republic*.

In 2003, the wreck of the *SS Republic* was discovered an amazing 1,700 feet (518 m) deep on the seabed about

Civil War artifacts like these were found on the *SS Republic*.

100 miles (161 km) off the coast of Georgia. Excavators from Odyssey Marine Exploration used advanced robotics to recover much of the cargo. They recovered more than 51,000 coins, plus thousands of artifacts that gave historians a better idea of life in the United States during the American Civil War.

JEANNETTE

Lieutenant George De Long set off in July 1879 from San Francisco, California, in his ship, the *Jeannette*, to lead the first expedition to the North Pole. He was determined to find an ice-free route through the Arctic Ocean.

At first, the *Jeannette*, a powerful coal-burning steamer, plowed through the fragments of ice in the water. But as the ship sailed northward, the ice became thicker and thicker. Lt. De Long altered the ship's course, hoping to find openings through the icy mass. By early September, the ice was refreezing around the ship as

quickly as the ship could break through it. The *Jeannette* was trapped in the ice. Around the ship, ice sheets scraped and crushed against each other.

As the months passed, the ice shifted, pushing against the ship and squeezing it. Eventually, the ice crushed the *Jeannette* and it sank. Lt. De Long and his crew escaped onto the ice just moments before the *Jeannette* disappeared beneath the surface.

Now they faced a long and dangerous trek on foot across the icy wasteland. Only 13 of the 33 explorers who set out for the North Pole returned home alive.

SOLO SAILORS

Some adventurous sailors take on the challenge of sailing alone, even around the world. The Vendée Globe is a nonstop around-the-world race alone in a sailboat. During the 1996–1997 Vendée Globe, the ocean presented some unexpected challenges for two competitors.

Englishman Tony Bullimore was sailing in his yacht, the *Exide Challenger*, across the Southern Ocean southwest of Australia when a storm hit suddenly. The waves were as tall as an eight-story building! Quickly, Bullimore clipped on his safety harness, took down the sails, and hurried down to the cabin below. But the mast broke and the boat rolled over and over. As freezing water flooded into the cabin, Bullimore set off the distress signal on his beacon and put on his insulated, waterproof sailing suit.

Bullimore stretched out on a narrow, dark shelf in the cabin that acted as an air pocket as the water level continued to rise inside the cabin. He had a few pieces of chocolate to eat and a little fresh water, and that was all.

After four days, rescuers finally found the yacht floating upside down—but there was no sign of life. When the rescue crew tapped on the upturned hull, a relieved Bullimore called out to them and swam out from beneath the boat to safety.

Meanwhile, French sailor Thierry Dubois got caught nearby in the same storm and his boat capsized several times. Dubois set off his beacon, put on his survival suit, and struggled out of the escape hatch. He tried to launch his life raft but a wave carried it away, so he clung to the rudder of his upturned yacht.

At last, an Australian search-and-rescue plane arrived and dropped a life raft, but again, a wave swept it away. The pilot dropped more rafts, but the stormy winds and towering waves made it difficult to reach the target. At last, Dubois managed

to climb inside a raft. There, he waited several days, eating emergency rations and reading a survival manual, until a frigate finally managed to make its way through the storm to rescue him.

Both solo sailors survived their ordeal—but only just.

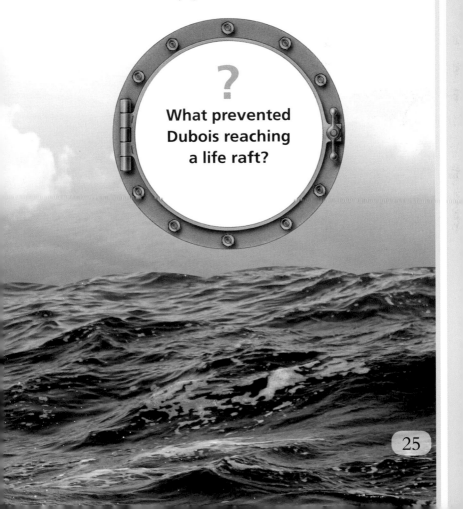

?
What prevented Dubois reaching a life raft?

TITANIC FACTS

Intended voyage: from Southampton, England, across the north Atlantic to New York City

Date: April 1912

Ship: 882 feet (269 m) long. The hull was divided into 15 bulkheads (vertical partitions) so that if one or two bulkheads flooded, the ship would still float—leading to the claim that the ship was "virtually unsinkable."

Passengers: 1,324 passengers (plus 898 crew). Many were emigrating to the United States. Strict divisions between 1st, 2nd, and 3rd class passengers meant that lower class passengers couldn't make their way to the lifeboat deck.

Weather: clear and calm, but cold

Collision: scraped against an iceberg, making several small cuts below the waterline, and flooding five of the bulkheads

Emergency procedures: with no emergency procedures, neither crew nor passengers knew where to go or what to do

Lifeboats: only 20 lifeboats, not enough for everyone, and some lifeboats were lowered into the water partly occupied

Rescue: after several hours in the lifeboats in the cold ocean without food or fresh water, surviving passengers were finally rescued by the *Carpathia*, a nearby ship

Seasickness

Don't let it ruin your voyage!

Symptoms

* Nausea
* Headaches
* Stomach cramps
* Dizziness
* Vomiting

Cause

Seasickness is a form of motion sickness, caused by the mismatch of information between your eyes and the balance system located in your inner ear. Your eyes detect that you are stationary, while your balance system senses motion.

Seasickness
Don't let it ruin your voyage!

How to avoid feeling seasick

✔ Keep busy and try to forget about it.

✔ Go out on the deck so you can adapt to being aboard the ship.

✔ Look at the horizon as a point of reference.

✔ Stay in an outside room with a window so you can see the horizon.

✔ The middle of the ship is more stable than the bow (front) or the stern (rear).

✔ Try a seasickness remedy, such as ginger candies, or wear a seasickness wristband.

✔ Foods such as ginger, green apples, and crackers may help reduce nausea.

! CARRY A SEASICKNESS BAG WITH YOU IN CASE ALL ELSE FAILS!

29

Chapter 2

Ships

Archaeological evidence proves that humans have been sailing the seas for more than 10,000 years. Ancient myths abound with seafaring heroes, such as Jason and his crew of Argonauts.

SAILING THROUGH TIME

Across time, ships have carried every imaginable kind of cargo. Ancient Greek and Roman vessels transported pottery jars filled with wine and olive oil and statues made of bronze and marble. Ornate Chinese boats called junks carried painted porcelain pots. In the 1600s, the Spanish fleets were loaded with gold and silver. Some ended up as shipwrecks, their precious cargo at the bottom of the sea.

Today, many different kinds of ships sail the oceans. These include cargo ships transporting goods from faraway factories, fishing boats, adventurers on sailboats or yachts, and cruise liners filled with vacationers. Most arrive safely at their destination ports.

However, experts estimate that more than 3 million shipwrecks lie on the ocean floor—but that's only a tiny fraction of the many sea voyages that have been made.

?

According to archaeological evidence, how long have humans been sailing the seas?

SAFER SHIPS

The ocean can certainly be a dangerous place, but with the use of modern navigational devices, it is probably safer now than it has ever been. Radar (radio detection and ranging) allows the ship's crew to see what is ahead even in the dark or in thick fog, while sonar (sound detection and ranging) and other echolocation devices enable sailors to

detect objects in the water below the ship.

Many of us use GPS (global positioning satellite) systems in our cars or on mobile phones. Global positioning satellites orbit the Earth and send down signals to help us find our way. Modern ships also use GPS to pinpoint their exact location anywhere in the world. Weather satellites provide information about storms and high winds so ships can avoid rough weather.

Modern luxury cruise ship

The bridge of a modern ship is the control center of the vessel. Most of the time, a ship's controls are on autopilot and computers steer the vessel on a steady course. Nevertheless, the ship's crew work in shifts so they can keep a close watch at all times in case something goes wrong.

The bridge is filled with radar screens, computerized charts, and other navigational aids. A receiver gathers signals from the GPS to give the helmsman who steers the ship accurate readouts of the ship's position.

Radar screens and other navigational aids on the bridge

Another way that ships are safer today is improved stability. Between the lower deck and the floor of the ship is a large open space called the hold. This is where cargo and ballast are stowed. Ballast is heavy material that keeps a ship stable at sea.

ON-BOARD HAZARDS

So, what can go wrong on board the ship and how can disasters be prevented? Firstly, the construction of the boat must be precise. For example, the welding of the metal hull must be absolutely watertight to avoid leaks. The cargo and ballast must be secured properly in the hold; otherwise, the balance of the ship could be skewed so that the vessel tips. Fire safety is also crucial and any fires must be put out immediately, ideally with a sprinkler system. Also of course, the captain and crew must ensure to plot the ship's course correctly.

In the past, a sailor's life was a dangerous one. Rocks could punch holes in a ship's hull; ice could crush it; wind and waves could overpower it. These and many other hazards could destroy vessels large and small. Mention "Davy Jones" to a sailor and it would send shivers down his spine. "Davy Jones" was a sailor's term for the bottom of the sea, where shipwrecks lie—a place that sailors wanted to avoid at all costs.

Jason and the Argonauts

LONG AGO IN ANCIENT GREECE, a young man called Jason arrived in the kingdom of Iolkos. He was determined to win back the throne that his uncle, King Pelias, had seized from his father many years before.

"Of course you may be king," Pelias told Jason, "if you retrieve the fleece of the golden ram from King Aietes, ruler of the distant kingdom of Colchis." Pelias gave an evil grin, for he knew that the golden fleece was guarded by a deadly serpent.

Jason had a fabulous ship built for the voyage and gathered many brave warriors to help him. The ship was called the *Argo*, and the warriors were the Argonauts. At last, Jason set off on his quest.

On the way, the Argonauts rescued a blind prophet called Phineus from the Harpies, wicked monsters who snatched people from Earth. In return, Phineus told Jason to release a dove into the sky as the ship approached the fearsome Clashing Rocks that guarded the entrance to Colchis.

Jason did and the rocks parted to let the *Argo* through. Jason went to claim the golden fleece.

"I will give you the golden fleece," said King Aietes, "if you harness two fire-breathing bulls to plow a field. Then sow the field with dragons' teeth—each of which will grow into a fierce warrior."

With the help of Medea, Aietes' daughter who had fallen in love with him, Jason completed the task. Still, Aietes wouldn't give up the fleece. Then Medea suggested he play music to lull the deadly serpent to sleep. It worked. At long last, Jason retrieved his prize!

Jason, Medea, and the Argonauts set sail for Iolkos, and after many more adventures, they arrived safely. Brave, determined Jason finally claimed his throne and ruled for many years.

# How does a Heavy Ship Float?

Climb into a bath of water and you'll notice the water level rise. The water is pushed aside, or displaced, to make space for you. More than 2,000 years ago, a Greek scientist called Archimedes found that the weight of water displaced by an object equals the weight of the object itself. However, an object weighs less in water because the upward force of the water, or buoyancy, partly supports the object.

This means that the downward force of a ship's weight has to balance with the upward force of the displaced water. The secret is that the hull of a ship takes up a lot of space, but its weight is less than the weight of the water it displaces, enabling the ship to float.

Try this experiment to see how the ship floats

You will need: glass marble; modeling clay; container of water

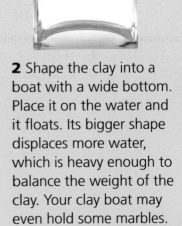

1 Drop the marble into the water. It sinks because the weight of the marble causes a downward force that is greater than the upward force of the water being displaced. Drop a ball of modeling clay into the water and it sinks, too.

2 Shape the clay into a boat with a wide bottom. Place it on the water and it floats. Its bigger shape displaces more water, which is heavy enough to balance the weight of the clay. Your clay boat may even hold some marbles.

41

CRUISE SHIP

WOULD YOU LIKE TO WORK ON A CRUISE SHIP?

You must:
- ✔ like traveling and meeting new people
- ✔ be able to handle long working hours
- ✔ NOT be prone to seasickness

All except top jobs require staff to share small cabins

The deck

Experienced sailors responsible for safe navigation
of the ship and everyone on board

CAPTAIN In charge of the entire ship and the safety of
all passengers

STAFF CAPTAIN Second in command to the captain

FIRST OFFICER Supervises the bridge

CHIEF RADIO OFFICER Responsible for the ship's
communications regarding weather, traffic, and safety

NAVIGATION OFFICER Navigates a safe route for the ship

QUARTERMASTER Keeps watch on the bridge and steers
the ship as directed by the officer in charge of the bridge

BOATSWAIN (also known as a bosun) Supervises ship maintenance and has a key role in mooring and anchoring

ABLE SEAMAN Performs routine ship maintenance and operates lifeboats and other safety equipment

Other cruise ship jobs

ENGINE DEPARTMENT Mechanics, engineers, plumbers, electricians, etc., keep the ship running in good order

ENTERTAINMENT DEPARTMENT Organize a wide range of on-board entertainment

ACTIVITIES AND YOUTH STAFF Plan passenger activities, including parties, games, etc., for children

MEDICAL STAFF Look after the health of everyone on the ship

CLEANING AND HOUSEKEEPING Take care of passengers and their cabins

SPA AND SALON STAFF Fitness instructors, hairdressers, manicurists, etc.

CATERING STAFF Chefs, servers, and dish-washers for on-board cafés and restaurants

RETAIL STAFF Managers and assistants for a wide variety of on-board stores

Chapter 3

OCEANS AND SEAS

Imagine you are on a boat in the middle of the ocean. You may be on a small sailboat or a yacht, or perhaps you're on an enormous cruise liner. All around the boat, you see a never-ending view of water and sky.

The surface of the water may be as smooth as glass, with not a wave or a ripple to be seen as your boat bobs along gently. Or perhaps the water is very choppy, with enormous waves that crash over your boat. Your voyage may include both calm seas and stormy seas, for no one can control the ocean.

OCEANS AND SEAS

Oceans cover more than two-thirds of the Earth's surface area. The Pacific is the biggest ocean. On its own, the Pacific Ocean takes up about one-third of our planet's surface. That's more than all of the land area on Earth combined. Although the name "Pacific" means peaceful, the Pacific Ocean is sometimes battered by violent storms.

Technically, large bodies of saltwater are called oceans, while smaller ones are seas. In reality, the oceans and seas all join to make one great big ocean.

The oceans form the world's biggest habitat for life, from the icy fringes of the frozen poles to the warm and magical coral seas of the tropics. Scientists believe that life on Earth probably began in these oceans, more than 3.5 billion years ago.

OCEAN ZONES

The Sun's warmth and light make the surface of the ocean warm and sunny, but the water gets colder and darker as you travel deeper. Life flourishes in the warm, sunlit surface waters of the sea. At least 80 percent of marine animals live within 660 feet (200 m) of the surface. Below the sunlit zone lies the twilight zone, where deep divers such as sperm whales hunt creatures of the deep. No sunlight at all penetrates through to the dark zone, below 3,300 feet (1,000 m), where luminous creatures glow in the darkness.

This compass jellyfish lives in coastal waters

WAVES AND CURRENTS

Seawater is constantly moving. At the surface, waves are formed by the action of wind blowing on the surface of the sea. Water spills over the top of the wave and breaks into a frothy spray. The highest waves are produced by strong winds blowing across the open ocean for long distances. Near the shore, wind drives the waves toward the beach, where they break when the water becomes too shallow.

Currents are huge masses of water moving through the oceans, both on the surface and deep below the surface. The currents take cold water from the polar regions toward the tropics where it warms up, and warm water from the tropics toward the poles where it cools down.

Wild Waves

The wind creates waves as it blows across the ocean's surface. As the wind gains strength, the ocean's surface gradually changes from flat and smooth to growing levels of roughness. Strong, persistent winds blowing over long distances form the biggest waves.

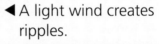

Wave Generation

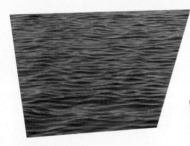

◄ A light wind creates ripples.

A stronger wind causes choppy water. ►

◄ Wind speeds over 40 mph (60 kph) can create very rough seas with waves 10 ft (3 m) high, or more.

▲ Chaotic waves

The area over which the wind blows is called the fetch. The ocean surface in the fetch is usually quite chaotic, with groups of waves of different sizes and wavelengths clashing and crashing. The stronger the wind, the more chaotic the waves become.

GEOGRAPHY OF THE OCEAN

In shallow water, a ship can easily be captured on banks of sand as the tide goes out. Currents in the sea cause sandbanks to shift constantly, so a boat's charts can only indicate roughly where they lie.

Ice in the Arctic Ocean

Ice is also a hazard. In the past, ships became trapped in the powerful grip of ice sheets created as seawater froze near the North and South Poles. Today, ice is more likely to be involved when it drifts into shipping lanes in the form of icebergs, as in the case of the *Titanic* in 1912.

COASTS

The coastlines where the land meets the sea can be sandy or rocky, or a mixture of the two. Coastlines are generally uneven, and sailors must look out for hidden dangers as they approach.

The powerful flashing beam of a lighthouse warns sailors that they should beware of rocks and helps guide them safely into harbor. When ocean fog make the lighthouse invisible, its loud horn sounds a warning.

Most lighthouses today are automatic, with a lamp surrounded by rotating lenses that concentrates the light so it is easier to see in the distance. A motor moves the lenses around the lamp and the beams scan the ocean, producing the characteristic flashes of the lighthouse.

Buoys are floating markers that indicate the position of known hazards. A chain or cable anchors the buoy to the seabed, and its shape and color identify the hazard it marks. Illuminated buoys warn of danger in places where it would be impossible to build a lighthouse.

SUBMERGED ISLANDS AND CORAL REEFS

An ancient story tells the tale of Atlantis, an island hidden beneath the sea. In reality, there are many islands concealed beneath the sea, perhaps cut off from the mainland by rising sea levels after ice ages, or created

by volcanic rock. These hidden islands can present a danger to ships, which may run aground or become damaged. These days, modern navigational devices such as sonar can enable sailors to detect submerged islands.

In tropical regions, a coral reef—built from the chalky skeletons of marine creatures—surrounds many islands. A coral reef needs clear, shallow seawater that allows sunlight to penetrate. Bigger ships anchor in deep water beyond the reef, but smaller vessels try to find their way through the sharp barrier. Not all succeed.

Coral covered by sea anemones in the Caribbean Sea

BERMUDA TRIANGLE

The Bermuda Triangle is a mysterious region in the south Atlantic Ocean where it is said that many unexplained air and sea disasters have occurred, including shipwrecks.

Christopher Columbus was among the first to recognize that the Bermuda Triangle was unusual. According to his log, on October 8, 1492, Columbus looked down at his compass and noticed that it was giving strange readings. Since then, sailors have been wary.

Many people believe that there are supernatural reasons for the disasters, while others think the reasons are scientific. Still others believe that disasters don't occur any more frequently in the Bermuda Triangle than elsewhere, considering the heavy shipping traffic in the area. Cargo ships and cruise ships pass through here on their way to ports in the

Americas, Europe, and the Caribbean. It's also a popular route for small pleasure craft on their way between the coast of the United States and the Caribbean.

We know that oceans and seas can be dangerous places—but is the Bermuda Triangle any more dangerous than other parts of the Earth's seas?

?

What happened to make Christopher Columbus think that the Bermuda Triangle was unusual?

The ancient Greek philosopher, Plato, told this story about 2,400 years ago. Is it true? Or is it a fable that teaches a lesson? **What do you think?**

ATLANTIS

POSEIDON, the great god of the sea, fell in love with Clito, a human woman, and built her a house on a high hill in the middle of an island. He made the island into a lush paradise, with fertile fields and tall forests, and surrounded it with rings of water and land. Clito and Poseidon had five sets of twins, all sons. The eldest, Atlas, eventually became king of the island, while the other sons became princes. The island became known as Atlantis.

The people of Atlantis lived in peace and prosperity. However, as generations passed, succeeding kings wanted to add to the wealth of the kingdom. The original home at the center of the island became a palace covered with gold. Bridges were built, connecting the rings of water and land to create a large city. A great harbor allowed riches to be imported to Atlantis from faraway places. The more the people of Atlantis had, the more they wanted. Once, they had lived together in harmony, but now greed and envy took over.

Poseidon decided to put a stop to it. The great god of the sea created a gigantic wave, even taller than the forest and higher than the high hill in the middle of the island. The gigantic wave crashed over the island, burying Atlantis beneath the ocean forever more.

Is Atlantis real? If so, where is it? Some people think it's beneath the Atlantic Ocean near the island of Bimini in the Bermuda Triangle. In 1968, an underwater causeway and building were discovered there. Although experts found that the Bimini Road causeway is a natural rock formation and the underwater building is from the 1930s, believers still think that energy crystals from Atlantis interfere with ships and aircraft in the Bermuda Triangle.

Location of Bermuda Triangle

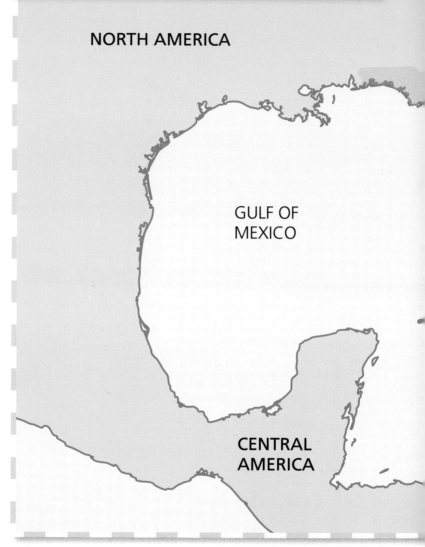

NORTH AMERICA

GULF OF
MEXICO

CENTRAL
AMERICA

62

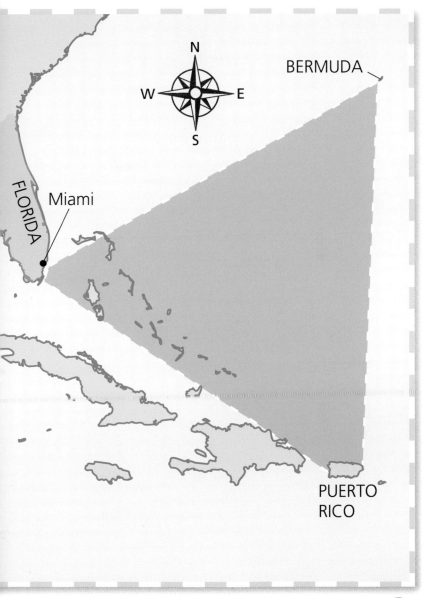

BERMUDA

FLORIDA

Miami

PUERTO
RICO

63

THE MYSTERY OF THE
BERMUDA TRIANGLE

The Bermuda Triangle is an area of about 500,000 square miles (1.3 million sq km). It is not marked on official maps and the United States Coast Guard "does not recognize the existence of the so-called Bermuda Triangle as a geographic area of specific hazard to ships or planes." However, many mysterious happenings have been reported there. These are just a few.

GHOST SHIP

Sailing through the Bermuda Triangle to Canada in 1881, the crew of the *Ellen Austin* spotted a ship in trouble. They were surprised to find no one on board. With some of the *Ellen Austin* crew sailing the ghost ship, they set sail together, but the ghost ship mysteriously disappeared in a bank of thick fog. When the *Ellen Austin* finally found the ghost ship, the crew had vanished.

Disappearing aircraft

Several months after the end of World War II in 1945, five Avenger torpedo bombers took off from Fort Lauderdale, Florida, over the Bermuda Triangle on a routine flying mission. The flight leader radioed for help, but the five aircraft and 14 crew members were never seen again. During the search mission, one of the searching aircraft also disappeared.

EERIE YELLOW HAZE

A group of experienced pilots flew a small aircraft through the Bermuda Triangle in 1986. Suddenly, the clear blue sky became an eerie yellow haze and the aircraft instruments stopped working. Through the thick haze, a narrow tunnel led to the sea below. After several hours, the eerie yellow haze suddenly vanished and they were surrounded once more by clear blue sky.

Gone fishing

In 2008, Phillip Fredericks set sail from St. John in the Virgin Islands, heading for Puerto Rico in his fishing boat. Despite having a powerful outboard engine, flares, life jackets, and two cell phones, Fredericks and his boat disappeared. Even after an intensive air and sea search by the United States Coast Guard, neither Fredericks nor the boat has ever been found.

65

BERMUDA TRIANGLE THEORIES

Are these incidents in the Bermuda Triangle the result of supernatural activity or is there another explanation?

Supernatural theories

The lost island of Atlantis

In ancient Greek myths, Atlantis was a great island civilization that sank beneath the sea. Some people believe it is near the island of Bimini in the Bermuda Triangle, and that traces of energy crystals from Atlantis can interfere with instruments on ships and aircraft.

Aliens and UFOs

Are aliens from other worlds kidnapping human beings from the Bermuda Triangle? This would explain the weird lights sometimes seen in the skies over the Triangle, and the disappearance of people without a trace.

Portal to another dimension

Is the Bermuda Triangle a portal linking this world with another dimension? Perhaps those who are missing have traveled to another time or place not usually accessible by earthlings.

Other theories

Gulf Stream
The Gulf Stream is a powerful ocean current passing through the Bermuda Triangle. It can make navigation difficult and sweep away the wreckage of ships, making them almost impossible to find.

Ocean floor maze
The ocean floor is a maze of shallow water and deep-sea trenches, plus many islands, including those that are submerged below the waterline and difficult to detect.

Magnetic mix-ups
The Bermuda Triangle is one of only two areas in the world where a magnetic compass points true north instead of magnetic north, making navigation more difficult.

Pirates
The area in and around the Bermuda Triangle has long been frequented by pirates. Could they be involved in the eerie happenings?

Wild weather
The Bermuda Triangle is known for rapid changes in weather. Hurricanes are common between June and November, while water spouts are quick but deadly tornadoes at sea that whip up water from the ocean's surface.

Methane gas
Pockets of concentrated methane gas are trapped under the ocean floor. When they erupt, the water becomes much less dense, creating a vacuum that could pull a boat under the surface, which might then be hidden by sediment on the ocean floor.

WHAT DO YOU THINK?

Chapter 4

WEATHER AT SEA

Among the greatest perils ships encounter at sea are the ones thrown at them by the weather. The ocean affects the weather, and vice versa. Sometimes, the ocean and the weather affect each other in quite extreme ways.

FOG

Fog is a cloud of tiny water droplets at or near the Earth's surface. Fog is more common over the ocean than on land because it picks up moisture from the water. Thick sea fog, formed when warm air blows across cold ocean water, causes very poor visibility. A vessel can lose its way and run aground, or collide with another boat. Before the invention of radar, thick fog made navigation extremely hazardous. Helmsmen (steering officers) had to rely on the sound of foghorns and ships' bells to avoid grounding or collisions.

WIND AND WAVES

Strong winds can whip up enormous ocean waves that wreak havoc on boats and ships. These powerful waves generally cause damage by swamping a craft with water, although they can also sometimes tip the boat over or even flip it upside down. Ships in the harbor, or that have run aground, must also beware the danger of being broken up by the pressure and suction of the waves crashing against the shore.

HURRICANES

Hurricanes are gigantic tropical storms that bring torrential rains, winds as fast as 150 miles per hour (240 km/h), and mountainous waves. Many hurricanes stay out at sea and never strike land.

Some hurricanes are powerful enough to pick up boats and throw them onto land or back into the sea. In the north Pacific, these severe tropical storms are called typhoons, while in the south Pacific and Indian Oceans, they are known as cyclones.

The Caribbean Sea is usually calm and sunny, but hurricane season can be fierce. An average season may mean up to a dozen tropical storms, with about half of these developing into full-fledged hurricanes. In 2008, the Caribbean Sea saw 16 tropical storms, including eight full-fledged hurricanes.

The Caribbean Sea is a popular location for passenger cruises, with enormous cruise liners heading down to the Caribbean Islands from nearby Florida and other places in North America. Cruise captains make passenger safety and comfort their top priority and therefore usually try to avoid storms. Sometimes, they try to outrun an approaching storm. While a storm moves at speeds of about 8 to 10 knots, a cruise ship can reach 22 knots. Cruise ships may also change their route to avoid a storm, or try to dock at the nearest port. However, it can be difficult to find an available port, especially if other ships are headed for the same port in the storm.

Despite advanced technology and careful precautions, sometimes it's impossible to prevent a ship from sailing into a storm. During Hurricane David in 1979, one cruise ship passenger described the feeling as if they went up 10 stories in

an elevator, then plummeted back down
again. Another cruise ship passenger sailing
through a hurricane described huge waves
crashing over the 10th floor and windows
being blown in. Hurricanes are a hazard
best avoided.

Make a Model Hurricane

A hurricane is the biggest and strongest of all storms, with powerful winds and torrential rain. It begins as a region of heated air over the warm waters of the tropics. The heated air expands and rises, creating an area of low pressure. As the surrounding air moves in toward the lower pressure, the Earth's rotation causes it to spin in a vortex. You can make a similar vortex in water.

You will need:
large bowl, water, spoon, pipette, food coloring

1 Fill the bowl with lukewarm water. Use the spoon to stir the water so it moves in a circle around the bowl, creating a vortex.

2 Release a few drops of food coloring into the center of the bowl. Watch the color move out and form bands—just like the clouds in a hurricane.

Hurricane facts

■ The size of a hurricane can be up to 400 miles (650 km) in diameter.

■ As more and more air is drawn into the storm, the wind speeds increase.

■ Conditions in the eye (center) of the storm are calm, while all around it are thick clouds and high-speed winds.

■ Wind speeds of 74 mph (118 km/h) are classified as hurricane-force, although wind speeds have been known to reach up to 210 mph (350 km/h).

■ Hurricanes become stronger as they move over warm water, but gradually fade out over cool water or land.

Terrible Tropical Storms

Hurricane season in the Caribbean is from June through November, but the season varies in different parts of the world. Much of the damage caused by hurricanes is a result of dramatic high tides called storm surges.

NAME **Typhoon Wipha**

LOCATION **Northwest Pacific**

DATE **2013**

WIND SPEED **131 mph (212 km/h)**

Record rainfall in Japan due to Typhoon Wipha caused deadly mudslides. As the typhoon moved northward, cold air turned the rain into a blinding snowstorm.

NAME **Cyclone Mahasen**

LOCATION **Bay of Bengal**

DATE **2013**

WIND SPEED **57 mph (93 km/h)**

Despite fading to a tropical storm by the time it made landfall, Cyclone Mahasen still led to devastating floods and landslides in parts of Asia.

NAME **Hurricane Katrina**

LOCATION **Louisiana**

DATE **2005**

WIND SPEED **140 mph (225 km/h)**

Storm surges broke through flood defenses in the city of New Orleans, causing flooding, which cost $108 billion worth of damage. The city's flood defenses have since been improved.

NAME **Hurricane Ike**

LOCATION **Caribbean Sea**

DATE **2008**

WIND SPEED **143 mph (230 km/h)**

In 2008, 16 tropical storms, including 8 full-scale hurricanes such as Ike, ripped through the Caribbean Sea, causing damage on many of the islands.

NAME **Typhoon Haiyan**

LOCATION **Philippine Islands**

DATE **2013**

WIND SPEED **235 mph (380 km/h)**

Between 20 and 25 tropical storms hit the Philippines every year, but Typhoon Haiyan was one of the worst, affecting 14 million people.

STORMY WEATHER
A storm rolls in across the ocean toward the shore, as a blanket of thick, gray clouds releases a torrent of rain.

Chapter 5

SURVIVAL AT SEA

The first thing a sailor needs in order to survive at sea is a reliable vessel. Alexander Selkirk, a sailor in the 18th century, understood this very well. When his captain insisted that the crew set sail in a ship that Selkirk knew was full of holes and therefore not seaworthy, he refused to board. Although he was left stranded by himself on a desert island, Selkirk's decision most probably saved his life. His adventures inspired the author Daniel Defoe's classic novel, *Robinson Crusoe*.

SHIPBUILDING

Today, shipbuilders make safety a top priority. For example, the design of a modern cruise liner involves high-tech software. This attempts to predict and resolve any potential safety problems before construction of the vessel even begins. The materials used in shipbuilding are strong and give the ship stability by keeping it light on the top and heavy on the bottom.

Below the waterline, the hull is divided into separate compartments by bulkheads. The watertight doors on the bulkheads are designed to prevent any leaks from spreading between compartments. Although the *Titanic* also had bulkheads, modern ships have the addition of sensors that monitor the hull for water and send warnings to the bridge. Any floodwater is redistributed around the ship through a piping system to keep the ship balanced.

EMERGENCY PROCEDURES

Since the sinking of the *Titanic*, international Safety of Life at Sea (SOLAS) regulations have been established. SOLAS requires passenger liners to hold safety drills known as muster drills, when the ship's crew explains emergency procedures and show passengers how to put on life vests.

The life vests inflate automatically to keep the wearer's head above water. A light and whistle are attached to the vest to attract attention.

In a real emergency, a muster alarm sounds—seven short whistles and one long whistle. Crew members immediately direct passengers to muster stations, designated areas where they gather for further instruction or to board lifeboats. The captain makes the ultimate decision as to whether to abandon ship.

"Mayday! Mayday! Mayday!"

In times of great danger, the captain and crew request help from all air and sea craft in the region by transmitting the international distress call. "Mayday" comes from the French "m'aidez," meaning "help me." It is always repeated three times. The Morse code "SOS" is also a recognized distress signal, although it is not as commonly used today.

LIFEBOATS

Lessons learned from the *Titanic* disaster mean that SOLAS regulations now require passenger ships to carry enough lifeboats for everyone on board. On large ships, lifeboats often hang from davits (launching cranes) on an upper deck. Passengers and crew climb aboard the boats, and a crew member, either on the deck or in the boat, lowers it into the water. This launching system is designed to work even if the ship has lost power or is tilting steeply.

Some cruise liners now use inflatable safety chutes similar to an aircraft evacuation system. Passengers and crew slide down feet-first into a large life raft.

Large, modern lifeboats of the sort you would find on a cruise liner can carry up to 250 passengers. Some lifeboats are inflatable. A canopy supported by an inflated tube protects those inside from harsh weather and high seas. A specially designed hull automatically rights the vessel if it capsizes in choppy water.

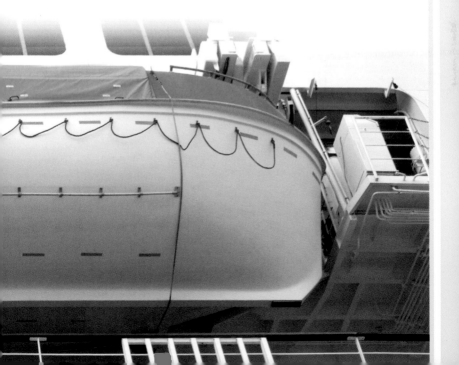

Most lifeboats also have engines, as well as flares to alert rescuers. On-board technology includes GPS (Global Positioning Satellite) and EPIRB (Emergency Position Indicating Radio Beacon). The EPIRB distress signal is picked up by satellites orbiting the Earth and relayed to rescue stations. Rescuers can then pinpoint a signal to within 984 feet (300 m).

A survival pack on the lifeboat usually provides food rations and fresh water. If these supplies run out, there is also fishing equipment and supplies to make sea water or even urine drinkable.

DANGERS AT SEA

When a ship sinks, the ordeal has only just begun for the survivors. The obvious dangers they face are drowning and freezing in cold seas. Along with life rafts, insulated, waterproof survival suits provide protection from these. They keep the wearer afloat and protected from the cold for up to six hours in freezing water.

Perhaps the cruelest potential hazard is lack of fresh water to drink if supplies run out. Even though a person may be surrounded by water, drinking the salty sea water makes the body dehydrated. It is better to drink nothing and wait for rain. Humans can survive for several months without food, but only about two weeks without fresh water—if they avoid losing moisture from sweating. Shelter is also crucial in hot climates as well as cold, because sunlight uses up vital water and burns and blisters skin.

"Water, water, everywhere, nor any drop to drink,"
is a famous line from the poem,
The Rime of the Ancient Mariner
about a sailor's adventures,
written by Samuel Taylor Coleridge in 1798.

TO THE RESCUE

To the world's lifeboat and air-sea rescue helicopter crews, it's all in a day's work to pluck people to safety from a stricken ship. They also rescue people from life rafts or pieces of floating wreckage, or they may fish them out of the water itself. These brave rescuers work in all weathers, knowing they could be the only hope for sailors in distress.

Good communication and speed are essential to all successful rescue efforts. As soon as a distress signal is picked up, a rescue operation swings into action. Coast guards pinpoint the location of the vessel with the help of satellites, and then pass the information to the rescue services who race to the scene as fast as they can. There are many different types of rescue lifeboats, ranging from inshore inflatables that are used for nearby rescues to large offshore lifeboats that can answer distress calls up to 50 miles (80 km) away.

Sometimes, lifeboats cannot reach more distant emergencies quickly enough, so helicopters fly to the rescue instead. Rescue helicopters can travel far greater distances than lifeboats, but the two often cooperate. A helicopter can speed injured passengers to the hospital faster, more safely, and more comfortably than a lifeboat.

But what happens if the vessel is so far from land that a lifeboat or helicopter can't reach it in time? In these cases, nearby ships will go to its aid, as when the *Carpathia* came to the rescue of the *Titanic* survivors.

?

What type of vehicle often cooperates with lifeboats in air-sea rescues?

Lifeboat equipment checklist

Modern lifeboats must carry a range of emergency equipment as specified by SOLAS. About 40–50 different items are required, depending on the type of lifeboat. Here are some of the items.

- ☑ Buoyant lifeline
- ☑ Whistle
- ☑ Searchlight
- ☑ Food rations and water
- ☑ Compass
- ☑ Fire extinguisher
- ☑ First aid kit
- ☑ Fishing kit
- ☑ Pocket knife
- ☑ Oars
- ☑ Sea anchor

Buoyant lifeline

Whistle

Searchlight

Food rations and water

Marine distress signals

Send an emergency signal to nearby boats and ships with a flare.

* Hand flare
* Rocket parachute flare
* Buoyant smoke signal

Hand flare

Buoyant smoke signal

Search and Rescue

Most modern lifeboats are fitted with EPIRB so rescue services can easily pinpoint their position.

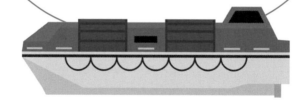

1 The EPIRB transmits a distress signal from the lifeboats to a satellite, probably one belonging to NOAA, which usually transmits weather information.

- **EPIRB**—Emergency Position Indicating Radio Beacon

- **NOAA**—National Oceanic and Atmospheric Association American agency that monitors changes to the environment, including weather and conditions at sea.

- **SARSAT**—Search and Rescue Satellite Aided Tracking Part of NOAA, the SARSAT system locates people in distress on land, at sea, and in the air.

2 The satellite pinpoints the location to within 164 feet (50 m) using GPS. Each EPIRB is licensed to a specific boat, so the satellite could also identify it.

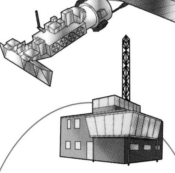

3 The location is relayed to the SARSAT Mission Control at NOAA's Satellite Operations Center in Maryland.

4 SARSAT Mission Control contacts the nearest United States Coast Guard Rescue Coordination Center, such as those located in Miami, Florida, and San Juan, Puerto Rico.

5 The Search and Rescue team is on its way!

Alexander Selkirk:
The Real Robinson Crusoe

In 1719, author Daniel Defoe wrote the classic adventure novel, *Robinson Crusoe*, about a man stranded on a deserted island. Experts believe that Defoe based his story on the adventures of Scottish sailor Alexander Selkirk....

AYE, so you want to know a wee bit about how I came to be stranded on my island. I was a good sailor, and a good navigator, though a bit hotheaded. In 1704, I was on the crew of a ship called the *Cinque Ports*. Captain Stradling was young and arrogant, only 21 years old—most of the crew had more sailing experience! We were privateers, hired by the British crown to raid Spanish ships and villages around the coast of South America.

When we discovered that worms were eating through the wooden ship, we docked on a deserted island for repairs. The ship was in a bad state and I told Captain Stradling that it wasn't seaworthy. Most of the crew seemed to agree, but Captain Stradling stood firm. We argued and I told Stradling that I'd rather stay on the deserted island than sail a leaky ship. I thought the crew would agree with me, but they all followed the captain back on board the ship. Stradling took great pleasure in leaving me stranded!

I expected to be found within a few days. In fact, it was five long years. I built a shelter near a stream, ate fish and wild goats, and foraged for fruit and vegetables. Oh, how I craved foods like bread and salt! I kept a close watch for ships on the horizon, though I hid if I saw a Spanish one. In time, I got used to life on my island, but it was still a joy when Captain Woodes Rogers rescued me in his ship the *Duke*!

I learned that the *Cinque Ports* had indeed sunk and only Captain Stradling and a few others had survived. So my sailor's instincts had saved me! When I returned to Britain, I became famous. I was interviewed for *The Englishman* magazine and became the inspiration for the best-selling novel, *Robinson Crusoe*.

AYE, BUT MINE IS THE TRUE TALE!

Chapter 6

Animal Heroes

Animals have always had a particular significance for sailors. Some sailors kept pets on board, such as dogs, cats, or rabbits. Animals sighted during the voyage symbolized the luck of the ship.

For example, dolphins swimming in front of a ship are considered good luck. Swallows are good luck birds if spotted at sea, but curlews and cormorants are bad luck birds.

In past times, many ships were known to carry a cat on board. Sailors often believed that the ship's cat could predict the weather. If the ship's cat sneezed, rain was forecast. If the cat was especially lively, there would be strong winds. Some sailors even thought cats had magic in their tails that caused storms at sea. Superstitions aside, animals have been known to play a part in shipwreck rescues.

DOG ON THE TITANIC

There were so many dogs on board the *Titanic's* maiden voyage in 1912 that a dog show had been scheduled for later in the journey. Sadly, the ship sank before the show could take place, but one special dog proved his courage during the disaster.

A big black Newfoundland terrier called Rigel belonged to the first officer, who went down with the ship. For three hours, Rigel swam around in the icy water looking for his master to no avail.

Then Rigel swam alongside one of the lifeboats. As the rescue ship, the *Carpathia*, approached, the lifeboat drifted under the bow, dangerously close to the big steamship. The crew of the *Carpathia* didn't know the lifeboat was in the water directly ahead and there was a chance the ship might plow right into them.

The *Titanic* survivors on the lifeboat were tired, cold, and hungry. They didn't have the strength to shout and alert the *Carpathia* crew of their whereabouts.

It was Rigel who swam ahead of the lifeboat, barking loudly. At last, Captain Rostron of the *Carpathia* heard him and noticed the lifeboat. Quickly, he ordered the engines stopped and the crew helped the survivors onto the *Carpathia*. They pulled the big black dog aboard too. Brave Rigel had led the lifeboat to safety.

?

How did Rigel the dog save the *Titanic* survivors in the lifeboat?

PORPOISES

In 1968, French sailor Bernard Moitessier took part in the first round-the-world sailing race. Four months into the race, he was steering his boat around a dangerous reef off Stewart Island, to the south of New Zealand. These reefs off Stewart Island are known as the South Trap because of the many ships that have foundered on them.

Dark clouds hid Moitessier's view of the island. Suddenly, a large school of porpoises appeared around his boat. They formed lines along the starboard (right) side of the boat and began rushing from the stern (rear) to bow (front) and then veering sharply to the right. They repeated this over and over again. Moitessier found their behavior most unusual. He'd never seen anything like it.

After watching the porpoises for a while, Moitessier checked his location. He was horrified to find that the wind had shifted and he was heading north—straight for the reef! As he altered course to the east, his boat swung sharply to the right. The porpoises' message now made perfect sense.

Now that the yacht was out of danger, the porpoises swam playfully around the boat. They stayed with Moitessier until he had safely passed the reef.

SAVED BY A SHARK

Taokai Teitoi believes he has a shark to thank for saving his life in 2012, after being lost in the Pacific Ocean for more than three months. The ordeal began after Teitoi and his brother-in-law, Ielu Falaile, were sworn in as police officers in the Kiribati capital of Tarawa. The country of Kiribati is made up of a series of islands. In order to get to their home on the island of Maiana, Teitoi and Falaile boarded their 15-foot (4.6-m) boat and set sail on a boat trip that should have taken two hours.

On the way, they stopped to do some fishing, and then fell asleep. When they awoke, they found that the boat had drifted so far off course that there were no longer any islands in sight. The boat soon ran out of fuel and the two men had no choice but to drift around in the open sea. They erected a cloth awning to protect them from the sun and ate fish that they caught from the sea. However, they had no fresh water to drink and after five weeks, Falaile died of dehydration. The very next day, it rained and Teitoi managed to fill two large containers with water.

Now Teitoi had fish to eat and fresh water to drink. He continued to drift in the ocean on his own. Once, he caught sight of a fishing boat, but the crew on the fishing boat didn't spot him. Weeks passed.

Then one day, after 15 weeks at sea, he was fast asleep under the awning when suddenly, he was woken by a sharp bump against the boat. Teitoi looked over the side to see a shark circling the boat and bumping against the hull. Then, he looked up and spotted a boat! It was near enough so that Teitoi could just make out the crew looking at him through binoculars. He waved frantically. The crew saw and came to rescue him.

Later, Teito told reporters, "If that shark hadn't nudged me awake, the crew of the boat might have thought I wasn't in trouble and might have sailed right past me."

Bottlenose Dolphins

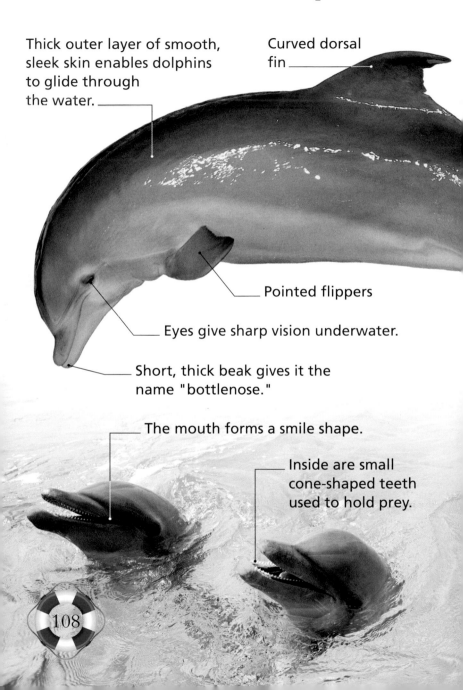

Thick outer layer of smooth, sleek skin enables dolphins to glide through the water.

Curved dorsal fin

Pointed flippers

Eyes give sharp vision underwater.

Short, thick beak gives it the name "bottlenose."

The mouth forms a smile shape.

Inside are small cone-shaped teeth used to hold prey.

Dolphin Facts

Length
6–13 feet (1.9–4m)

Weight
can be up to
1,100 lbs (500 kg)

Color
light blue to slate gray
with pale underside

The tail is
called a fluke.

■ Dolphins are mammals. They breathe air, but can stay underwater for 4–5 minutes.

■ A female dolphin is a "cow." A male is a "bull" and a baby is a "calf."

■ A group of dolphins is a "pod" or "school." There can be 10–100 dolphins in a pod.

■ Bottlenose dolphins live in oceans and seas around the world, except for polar regions. They eat a varied diet of fish, squid, and shellfish.

■ They can leap high into the air in a move called a "breach" and slap the water with their tails. This may be a form of communication or simply playful behavior.

■ These curious, intelligent animals are known to interact with humans.

■ Dolphins often swim alongside ships, using the waves created by the ship to conserve energy.

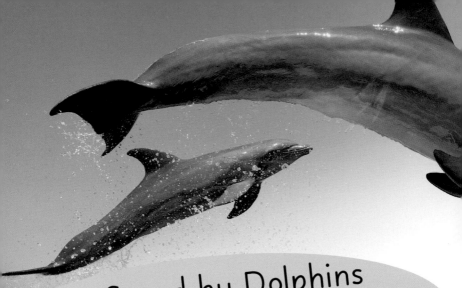

Saved by Dolphins

Read these experiences of people who have been saved by dolphins. These are all true stories, EXCEPT for one. Which experience is false?

See page 125 for the answer.

DOLPHIN RESCUES BOY

In 2000, Davide Ceci fell out of his father's fishing boat off the coast of Italy. Davide didn't know how to swim, but was saved when a dolphin pushed him up out of the water toward the boat so his father could pull him back in to safety.

DOLPHINS SHOW THE WAY

In 2004, 12 scuba divers were swept away from their boat in the Red Sea. Rescuers searched but couldn't find them—until a group of dolphins jumped over the prow of the rescue boat, all in the same direction. They followed the dolphins and found the scuba divers.

DOLPHINS KEEP DIVER AFLOAT
In 2006, Matthew Harvey was knocked unconscious while scuba diving. After about 56 hours in the water, the crew of a passing yacht spotted him, surrounded by dolphins who were apparently keeping him afloat.

DOLPHINS SAVE SURFER
Todd Endris was surfing off the coast of California in 2007 when a shark attacked him. Then a pod of dolphins swam up and surrounded him, protecting him from the shark until he was able to surf back to the safety of the beach.

DOLPHIN HERO
In 2008, an eyewitness in the Philippine Islands saw a large dolphin push fisherman Joseph Cesdorio onto the shore in an attempted rescue after his fishing boat capsized in a typhoon. Sadly, neither Cesdorio nor the dolphin survived the ordeal.

DOLPHIN RIDE
In 2015, Juan Rivera and his sister, Felicia, had drifted far away from the beach in Mexico. Suddenly, two dolphins nudged the children with their beaks. Juan and Felicia climbed onto the dolphins' backs, who gave them a ride safely back to the beach.

Chapter 7

Exploring Shipwrecks

Some shipwrecks are abandoned beneath the sea or grounded near beaches, often rotting under the elements of nature. Some are historically significant and may even be protected by UNESCO (United Nations Educational, Scientific, and Cultural Organization). Some shipwrecks have been turned into tourist attractions. Many others are hidden beneath the sea, never to be found.

In the past, some wrecks were too deep and inaccessible. Developments in diving and salvage technology mean that wrecks can now be reached at greater depths than ever before. Scientists and salvage experts can locate and map sites without even getting their feet wet. If they can find out what caused a modern wreck to sink, they can try to make sure it doesn't happen again. An ancient wreck can provide information about past times. Sometimes, the main reason for exploring shipwrecks is simple curiosity.

LOCATING THE WRECKS

Locating the site of a shipwreck is often tricky. Coast guards can give searchers the last known position of a modern vessel. For old ships, wreck-hunters must search for clues in old maps and charts. The only ways to confirm the location is to swim down to the seabed, scan it with a sonar device, or use a submersible vehicle equipped with lights and cameras.

Occasionally, wrecks are found by accident. They can be discovered by pleasure divers, tourists on a beach at low tide, or fishermen when their nets catch on a submerged object.

Flotsam is the floating wreckage of a shipwreck. It may be carried far away by waves and wind. Often, the high tide brings flotsam to the shore. The next time you find a piece of driftwood on the beach, think about where it came from. Was it part of a shipwreck?

SHIPWRECK TRAIL

One of the most famous places to explore shipwrecks is the Shipwreck Trail around the islands off the tip of Florida called the Florida Keys. Nine ships lie in the sand around the coral reefs a few miles offshore. Visitors may dive down and explore, but they must not disturb the wrecks or take any artifacts. The trail lies in the Florida Keys National Marine Sanctuary, so divers must also be careful to preserve the habitat of coral reefs.

Wrecks on the trail include the *San Pedro*, part of a fleet of 22 ships sailing from Cuba to Spain with a cargo ranging from silver coins to Chinese porcelain. Most of the fleet sank during a hurricane in 1733. The trail also has more modern wrecks, such as some that were intentionallly sunk in the 1980s to act as artificial reefs that encourage the coral to grow.

DIVING DOWN

Once a shipwreck has been located, it's time to dive down and learn more about it. Scuba divers swim in lightweight rubber wetsuits, breathing oxygen from tanks strapped to their backs. Invented by French ocean explorer Jacques Cousteau in 1943, scuba stands for "Self-contained Underwater Breathing Apparatus." Scuba divers can swim to depths of about 330 feet (100 m), or if sealed inside a special atmospheric diving suit (ADS), they can work at depths of 2,000 feet (610 m).

For wrecks that are too deep for divers to reach, submersible vehicles are used. Some submersibles are manned and can stay underwater for up to ten hours. Inside, divers are protected from the huge pressure of water at the depths of the ocean. Other submersibles are remotely operated vehicles, controlled from a ship on the surface. Robots with artificial intelligence are called automated underwater vehicles. They can stay underwater for several months.

RAISING A WRECK

For salvors, archaeologists, and treasure hunters, long-lost cargo is the ultimate underwater discovery. Over time, shipwrecks and their contents may become buried in mud and sand on the seabed, hiding them. But this sediment also helps preserve wooden boats, by keeping out the oxygen, which would otherwise speed up the decay of the timbers. On the other hand, metal ships are badly corroded by seawater. In shallow water, algae and sometimes coral may grow on a wreck, turning them into artificial reefs. Inside a wreck, fish often shelter as if in an underwater cave.

When archaeologists and accident investigators find shipwrecks, they sometimes decide to raise them for detailed investigation. It is important to first record where each object rested on the seabed, as this information can reveal a lot about what happened to the ship. Divers spend much of their time underwater measuring, mapping, sketching, and taking photographs.

Once they have recorded the area, lighter objects are raised with the help of an airlift—a buoyant air-filled bag. Salvage vessels fitted with cranes are then used to raise the wreck itself to the surface. The ship and its artifacts are cleaned and studied. They may be put on display in museums so that people like you can find out more about the passengers and crew of shipwrecks, the times they lived in—and how the ships ended up at the bottom of the ocean.

Ring and gold coin from a pirate shipwreck

Surviving at Sea Game

1	Having a fantastic cruise Go forward 3 spaces.	3	Spot dolphins breaching. Go forward 2 spaces.	5
Thick sea fog means you skip a turn.	**19**	A fresh sea breeze moves you forward 5 spaces.	**17**	**16**
21	You've sailed into a hurricane! Go back 3 spaces.	**23**	The ship crashes into a submerged island. Go back 8 spaces.	**25**
You're in the eye of a hurricane. Skip a turn.	**39**	The lifeboat is equipped with EPIRB and GPS. Go forward 7 spaces.	**37**	**36**
41	Spot another lifeboat nearby. Go forward 5 spaces.	**43**	Rations on the lifeboat run out. Skip a turn.	**45**
Land ahoy! You've made it to safety. Good job!	A sandbank blocks your way. Go back 9 spaces.	**58**	**57**	**56**

Who will reach safety first?

To play, you will need: counters for each player and a die.

6	**7**	You're sailing through the Bermuda Triangle! Go back 5 spaces.	**9**	Skip a turn while you investigate a possible UFO.
15 You're feeling seasick. Go back 7 spaces.		**13**	Choppy seas. Go back 3 spaces.	**11**
26	**27**	The captain gives the order to abandon ship. Skip a turn.	**29**	You paid attention at the muster drill and put on your life vest. Go forward 5 spaces.
35 Your flare can't be seen in bad weather. Go back 8 spaces.		**33**	You board the lifeboat quickly and safely. Go forward 4 spaces.	**31**
46	**47**	A strong wind blows you off course. Go back 2 spaces.	**49**	**50**
55 Pod of dolphins shows the way to the island. Go forward 2 spaces.		**53**	**52**	It's clear, sunny weather. Full speed ahead! Go forward 4 spaces.

Take turns rolling the die. Follow the instructions in the squares. The player who reaches the island first wins the game.

Shipwreck Quiz

Can you find the answers to these questions about what you have read?

1. What is the rear of the ship called?

2. In which year did the Titanic sink?

3. What does "Pacific" mean?

4. In the ancient Greek myth, what is the name of Jason's ship?

5. Where can you visit the *Vasa* shipwreck?

6. Which race were Tony Bullimore and Thierry Dubois sailing in when their yachts capsized?

7. What does SOLAS stand for?

8. What is another name for the center of a hurricane?

9. How many whistles is a muster alarm?

10. Two of the three points of the Bermuda Triangle are Miami, Florida and Bermuda. What is the third point?

11. What is a group of dolphins called?

12. What is a severe tropical storm called in the South Pacific?

13. What creates waves in the ocean?

14. Alexander Selkirk's story is said to be the inspiration for which classic book of 1719?

15. What kind of animal saved Taokai Teitoi when he was stranded at sea?

16. What does EPIRB stand for?

17. What is the name of the island that the Greek philosopher Plato said was buried beneath the ocean?

18. Where is the Shipwreck Trail?

Answers on page 125.

Glossary

Archaeological
Relating to the study of the remains of past human life.

Autopilot
Controlled or driven by computers.

Beacon
Signal, such as a light or radio signal.

Cargo
Goods being transported.

Crow's nest
High platform on a ship's mast used as a lookout.

Detection and ranging
Finding an object and measuring its distance,
as in radar and sonar.

Echolocation
Locating an object using the sound waves that
the object reflects back.

Embark
To start a journey.

Equator
Imaginary line across the middle of the Earth, dividing
it into Northern and Southern Hemispheres.

Knot
The speed in water, one nautical mile per hour.

Navigate
To direct the route from one place to another,
often using maps or instruments.

Seaworthy
Safe for a sea voyage.

Submerged
Under the surface of the water.

Submersible
Vessel used to explore under the ocean.

Tropical
Relating to hot regions of the Earth just north and just south of the equator.

Vessel
Any boat or ship.

Vortex
Air or water whirling around the center of a circle, such as a whirlwind or whirlpool.

Waterline
Line marking the level of the water on a boat or ship.

Answer to pages 110–111: Dolphin Ride

Answers to the Shipwreck Quiz:
1. Stern; **2.** 1912; **3.** Peaceful; **4.** *Argo*; **5.** Stockholm, Sweden; **6.** Vendée Globe (around-the-world race); **7.** Safety of Life at Sea; **8.** Eye of a hurricane; **9.** Seven short whistles and one long whistle; **10.** San Juan, Puerto Rico; **11.** Pod or school; **12.** Cyclone; **13.** Wind; **14.** Robinson Crusoe; **15.** Shark; **16.** Emergency Position Indicating Radio Beacon; **17.** Atlantis; **18.** Florida Keys.

Index

ballast 35–36
Bermuda Triangle 58–59, 61–67
bow 7, 16, 100, 102

captain 11, 17, 36, 42, 73, 85, 96–97
cargo 16, 18–19, 30–31, 35–36, 58, 118
Caribbean 5, 57, 59, 72, 78–79

hull 7, 9–11, 17, 23, 26, 36–37, 40, 83, 106
hurricane 18, 71–72, 74–79

ice 20–21, 37, 53
iceberg 9–11, 27, 53

lifeboat 11, 17, 26–27, 86–88, 90–94, 100–101
liner 8, 10, 16, 31, 44, 72 83–84, 87

maiden voyage 10, 12, 100

North Pole 20–21

Pacific Ocean 46, 71, 104
port 7, 17, 31, 58, 73

sailor 22–25, 32, 37, 54, 58, 82, 96–99, 102
steamship 18, 20, 100
stern 6, 102
storm 22, 24–25, 33, 45–46, 71–74, 81, 99

Titanic 8–11, 26, 53, 83–84, 86, 91, 100

vessel 16, 30, 34, 36–37, 57, 69, 82–83, 87, 90–91, 114, 119

waves 22, 24, 37, 45, 48, 50–51, 70, 75, 114
wind 12, 24, 33, 37, 48, 50–51. 70, 76–77, 103, 114

yacht 22, 24, 31, 44, 103, 111

About the Author

Caryn Jenner writes and edits a variety of books for children of all ages, including both fiction and non-fiction. For DK Publishing, she has written *Eyewitness Workbook: Earth*, as well as several titles in the *DK Readers* series and *In the Shadow of the Volcano* for *DK Adventures*. Her picture book, *Starting School*, was one of the eight books longlisted for the UK's 2012 School Library Association Information Book Award in the Under 7s age group.

Caryn also teaches English to speakers of other languages and volunteers at a local school. She grew up in the USA, but has made her home in the UK for many years. She lives in London with her husband, daughter, and three cats.

About the Consultant

Dr. Linda Gambrell, Distinguished Professor of Education at Clemson University, has served as President of the National Reading Conference, the College Reading Association, and the International Reading Association. She is also reading consultant to the *DK Readers*.

Have you read these other great books from DK?

DK ADVENTURES

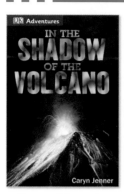

Mount Vesuvius erupts in this adventure. Will Carlo escape?

It's a life-or-death adventure as the gang searches for a new home planet.

Chase twisters in Tornado Alley in this pulse-racing action adventure.

Experience ancient Roman intrigue in this time-traveling adventure.

Emma adores horses. Will her wish come true at a riding camp?

Lucy follows her dream... Will she make the cut?